SEP

2008

I Do . . .

I Do...

Questions for the Biggest Day of Your Life

Evelyn McFarlane & James Saywell

Villard / New York

Published in the United States by Villard Books, an imprint of The Random House
Publishing Group, a division of Random House, Inc., New York.

VILLARD and "V" CIRCLED Design are registered trademarks of Random House, Inc.

Library of Congress Cataloging-in-Publication Data
McFarlane, Evelyn.
I do: questions for the biggest day of your life / Evelyn McFarlane & James Saywell;
illustrations by Evelyn McFarlane.
p. cm.
ISBN 978-0-345-50414-2 (hardcover : alk. paper)
1. Weddings—Planning. I. Saywell, James. II. Title.
HQ745.M395 2008
395.2'2—dc22
2008002508

Printed in the United States of America on acid-free paper

www.villard.com

2 4 6 8 9 7 5 3 1

First Edition

BOOK DESIGN BY MARIA ELIAS

 SEP   2008

Dedicated to my parents, who, after forty-seven years of
matrimony still have a marriage one would dream of.

—Evelyn

And to mine, two soul mates who have proved marriage
can be a dream come true.

—James

Introduction

Do you take this man . . . Do you take this woman . . .

If there are a number of days in one's life that could be described as life-changing, a wedding day is surely one of the biggest. Yes, graduation day is unforgettable, and the birth of a child is unequaled, and sadder occasions, like the passing of a loved one, are momentous. But a wedding day is truly special. Filled with optimism, with just about all the hopes packed together with anticipation into a single ceremony on a single day. It is the occasion when everyone we know and love celebrates a choice that we have made about a single person we cherish more than anyone. A single person we have decided to meld our life with. A person we love more than ourselves.

During the engagement period the planning for this giant day can be bumpy and nerve-wracking, but it can also be fun, thrilling, and emotional. So many decisions to be made, plans to hatch, and details to consider, all designed to add up to the day you've long dreamed of . . . a day for the two of you. With so many questions along the way, why not fantasize as well as plan; why not imagine as well as decide?

I Do . . . is the book that collects all those questions into an adventure of fun, enlightenment, and conversation. Raising issues, reminding of duties, pointing out humor, recognizing seriousness. And discovering a little bit more about yourself and your fiancé along the way. *I Do* . . . is a book to be read by any and every bride and groom, together or individually. It's a book to be passed around at the bridal shower, read aloud at the rehearsal dinner, cited at the stag party, and shared by all who will be involved in the big event.

Are you trying to make this wedding unique to the two of you? Do you care about "keeping up with the Joneses"? Are you searching for themes for the shower or reception? Do you wish your fiancé would get more involved in the decision making? Are you stumped by some of the planning details?

Open this book at any page and ask yourself a question. Ask your betrothed, or a loved one, or your best friend. See how different people answer the same question and who has the most surprising responses. Only by asking do we find our own answers, and understand our dreams and desires. And the journey is awfully good fun. Most of all, we hope this collection adds to the unique joy of getting married. Congratulations!

I Do . . .

How would you finish the sentence
"A perfect wedding day is . . ."?

When you close your eyes and envision the atmosphere of your wedding, what one word describes it best?

❧

How does your *ideal* number of wedding guests measure up to the *actual* number of guests that you can invite?

❧

You wish your parents could understand one thing better about your fiancé. And it is . . . ?

❧

The person you most dreaded telling that you were engaged was who?

What do you hope will happen every year on your wedding anniversary?

Who will be calling the shots in the planning of your wedding, and who will meddle most?

❧

If you were to use three adjectives to describe the bridesmaids' outfits, what would they be?

❧

Who was the person from your fiancé's family you were most nervous about meeting for the first time?

❧

If your dad could not give you away, who would you have do it?

If you could spend your wedding night in the
honeymoon suite of any hotel in the world,
where would you go?

What one thing from the wedding ceremony do you hope to preserve, to hand down to your own children?

❧

If you could change one habit of your beloved before marrying, what would it be?

❧

What friend do you trust most to run cover for you on your wedding day if you need help?

❧

If you could read the mind of your spouse during the "I do" moment of your wedding, what would you like him/her to be thinking?

What part of the big day will be most
important for your mom, and what part for
your dad?

If you could dance like anyone for the first dance, who would it be?

❧

You have decided that on your wedding night you will tell your fiancé one thing he/she doesn't know about you. What will it be?

❧

Two people who should *not* sit beside each other at the reception dinner are?

❧

At what points during the big day will you be able to relax and be yourself, and at what points will you feel you need to be playing a role?

You knew she was the One when...?

You know he is Mr. Right because...?

You wish two people could get along well just for the week of your wedding. Who?

❧

Now that you are engaged and planning a ceremony you discover that your religious values are different than your fiancé's. What do you do to reconcile the differences?

❧

The thing you have had the easiest time agreeing on so far has been what?

❧

What one detail of the big day do you think about and worry about most?

Your dream wedding cake has the flavor of . . .

the shape of . . .

the look of . . .

and the topper is?

What song would you love to have played and dedicated
to your parents at the reception?

✎

Who, without a doubt, will give you the strangest
wedding gift of all?

✎

Your friends and family tell you the dress you love
is quite unflattering on you. What do you do
with their advice?

✎

Do you believe there are really such things as auspicious
days or bad luck days for weddings?

If both of you were to separately interview a
wedding planner, what is the first question
each of you would ask?

If you could plan a number of little surprises and events throughout the reception to keep the guests entertained, what would they be?

∽

You would love to have one thing said about you in the toast. What would you like to hear?

∽

If you were to finish the phrase "the key to our relationship is . . . ," how would you complete it?

∽

If you started to have doubts about getting married, who is the first person you would turn to for help?

A famous photographer wants to take your wedding photos and publish them in one magazine. What photographer do you want, and which magazine would you like to be in?

The caterer has suggested that the bartender offer a specialty drink to go with your theme and atmosphere. What do you envision?

❧

If you were to name the wedded couple of your dreams— two people you truly admire—who would they be?

❧

Which of the flower arrangements will be the most important and where will it be placed?

❧

If you were to name one food that must be served at the reception, and one that should never be served, what would they be?

You decide together on three gifts that you know you want from guests. What are they?

If you were to finish the phrase "I would cancel the wedding for sure if . . . ," how would it end?

❧

You can have any famous chef or foodie plan your menu. Who do you choose?

❧

Do you think strangers who attend your wedding as dates should sign the guest book?

❧

Under what conditions would you re-throw the bouquet?

You find out that you will be pregnant and showing for the wedding day. Do you buy a dress that hides it or celebrates it? Do you both agree on this?

Who will be perfect to help the photographer take the necessary photos of important friends and family during the reception party?

❧

A great way to keep children entertained at the reception is . . . ?

❧

If you could have any performer perform live at your reception, who would you choose?

❧

If you could have the invitations printed on, and put in, something other than paper and envelopes, what would you choose?

Your mom wants to go to your bachelorette
party. What do you do?
Your dad wants to come to your stag party.
What do you tell him?

23

How much do you each plan to drink at the reception?

❧

Getting married can affect relationships with your single friends. How will yours change?

❧

If you decided to have two officiants perform the ceremony, who would be the perfect pick for each of you?

❧

At the reception, ideally, how much time will you plan to spend together, side by side, and how much time will you want to socialize by yourself with the guests?

What surprising behavior has emerged from your fiancé since the announcement of your engagement?

If you could have wedding crashers at your reception,
who would you want to surprise you?

❧

In what way will you be "keeping up with the Joneses"
with regard to all the planning and the details of
this event?

❧

It is two days before the wedding and the favors have not
arrived. What is your backup plan?

❧

What is the most you would each spend on a dress and
attire for the wedding day?

What part of the whole engagement process do you wish could last forever, and what part will you be glad is over?

27

All eyes are on you while walking down the aisle. What will you be thinking, and what do you want them to see?

❧

What Web site would you love to podcast your wedding on?

❧

You've decided to set up a bride and groom's Web page. What do you call it and what's on it?

❧

Your fiancé has better taste than you in what? And worse taste than you how?

❧

If your future father-in-law asked you to show him details of your financial position, how would you react?

In what ways are you both more connected,
and in what ways less, since you became
engaged?

If you could exercise an isolated part of your body, intensely, in preparation for the wedding, what part would it be?

❧

What is your idea of a great rehearsal dinner, and how late do you plan on staying out that night before the wedding day?

❧

What would you love to say to your father while walking together down the aisle before he gives you away? And what do you want to hear from him?

❧

The moment you believed that your spouse-to-be truly loved you was when?

What is the biggest DO and biggest DON'T
of wedding guest etiquette?
What are the biggest DO's and biggest
DON'Ts of wedding host etiquette?

What activity that does not include you, do you hope
your spouse continues after marriage?

⌯

You want your betrothed to give up one hobby after you
get married. Which one?

⌯

Your father strongly advises keeping your assets separate
upon marriage, but your spouse-to-be wants to join
all finances. What do you do?

⌯

If you could have one piece of news delivered on the
morning of the wedding, what would you want to hear?

In a word, what kind of bride do you want to be?
What does it take to be a great groom?

How do you foresee being carried, or carrying the bride, over the threshold?

✎

Where is the line between comfort and fashion with regard to this day?

✎

What one thing could happen to truly make this the wedding of your dreams?

✎

Have you ever suffered from bride envy?

✎

What does the engagement ring symbolize for you?

You have just learned you are going to inherit a large amount of money before getting married. How will this affect your prenuptial?

If someone offered you an unlimited amount of money to call off your wedding, how much money would it take for you to consider it?

❧

Your mother-in-law-to-be says the one thing that will make her eternally happy is to plan and host your wedding. How do you respond?

❧

What one thing do you secretly plan on changing about yourself after this marriage?

❧

What is your policy going to be on kids attending the wedding?

❧

You can have any designer make your fantasy wedding dress. Who do you commission?

Who do you predict will wear the best and
worst outfits to your affair?

If you could be as sexy as anyone, famous or otherwise, on your wedding day, whose sex appeal would you want?

❧

Your bride shows up the morning of the wedding with far too much makeup on. What do you say?

❧

If making the parents happy was not factored into your wedding preparations and plans, what would you do differently?

❧

If you were going to commission an ice sculpture, what figure would you have carved?

Your groom surprises you in one way the night before the wedding. What would you like the surprise to be?

Your fiancé and your mother have a big fight about the planning. How do you handle it?

✧

If you could have asked your own parents one thing the day before *their* wedding, what would it be?

✧

If you *had* to take someone with you on your honeymoon, who would you choose?

✧

Your buddies arrange the lap dance of your dreams for your bachelor party. Who does the honors?

✧

Your mates are planning the stag party for you. What do you pray will not happen?

You find out your fiancé had used the
same ring to propose to somebody else.
What do you do?

Who are you most worried about offending the week of the wedding?

❧

You are going to prepare an emergency kit to have handy on your wedding day. What items do you include?

❧

The person you want to impress most at this wedding is . . . ?

❧

What decisions do you want to make alone and which should definitely be made together in this engagement period?

❧

You'd love to have someone famous at the party. Who?

If you could have the blessing of any one figure, religious or otherwise, who would you choose?

What will be the hardest part of dealing with your future mother in-law?

∽

If you could have one small item delivered with each of the invitations, what would it be?

∽

If your fiancé canceled the wedding, what would you do about the ring?

∽

You are going to devise a test of your fiancé's faithfulness. What does it involve?

You have a chance to go into your fiancé's
e-mail and bookmarks while he/she is away,
without getting caught. What do you do?

You have asked your fiancé never to bring up one subject with your parents and your parents never to bring up one topic with your fiancé. What are they for each?

❧

Your fiancé can't stand one of your best friends and asks you to give up the friendship after you wed.
What do you do?

❧

If you could have customized wedding boxers, what would they have printed on them?

❧

You want to choose the wedding favor for men and for women that best fits with your day. What can they be, and why are they perfect?

You just don't care if you break the standard
wedding rule when it comes to . . .

You can alter one aspect of your body to help make
your wedding dress look more elegant. What
do you change?

❧

Your fiancé tells you it is necessary to reschedule
the honeymoon due to a business trip.
How do you react?

❧

If your fiancé had to move to another country for work
and asked you to wait for the wedding, what is the limit
of how long you would wait?

❧

If you could have any famous movie director film your
wedding, who would you pick?

What are the best and worst wedding day
stories you know?

You arrange to have a little surprise waiting on the pillow of your betrothed the night before the wedding. What is it?

❧

Your fiancé suddenly has a change of mind, and wants a prenup, what do you think?

❧

Your fiancé has asked you to get rid of all photos of former lovers before you get married. Will you?

❧

If you could have one last night together with anyone, other than your fiancé, who would it be with?

❧

You want one person to just "back off" about one thing. Who is it and why?

You want this marriage to be most like your
parents' in one way and least like theirs
in another. Which is it for each?

You have both decided to set a number of hours aside for personal time each week when you are married. How many hours will it be for each of you?

❧

If you were to list the three top priorities for the planning of the event, what would they be and who is in charge of them?

❧

You want to veto a song to make sure it does not get played during the wedding. Which one?

❧

You get an expensive but appalling gift from your in-laws. What do you do?

If you could go on a "money is no object"
honeymoon, where would you go and
for how long?

If there is one person or couple you'd rather *not* invite to your wedding—but will—who is it?

❧

Your bride whispers one thing in your ear just before saying "I do." What would you love her to say?

❧

If you were to come up with a term other than "tie the knot" to describe your engagement, what would it be?

❧

The top picks for the theme of your bridal shower are . . . ?

What have you found to be the biggest
difference between a male approach to a
wedding and a female approach to a wedding?

What is *your* perfect hair-day for this event?

∾

You had the picture of the ideal person to marry years ago. How does it compare to the person you are marrying now?

∾

You want an invitation that reflects the two of you. What adjectives would you use to describe the look?

∾

What is the best strategy for getting the groom involved and genuinely excited in the planning?

Your fiancé has agreed to sit down to give frank input regarding the preparations. What are the first three questions you ask?

You are offered unlimited skin care products from any company for the whole month leading up to the wedding. Which brand do you choose?

✺

If you could have your dream registry, where would it be, and what would you list?

✺

There are some friends of your fiancé that you are looking forward to spending more time with, and some you are not. Who is it for each?

✺

What will the cell phone policy be for both of you at the ceremony, the reception, the wedding night, and the honeymoon?

If you could learn to do one new thing before
the wedding, what would it be?

If your fiancé had a brief fling during the engagement, would you want to know?

❧

You must describe to the photographer the look you want for the wedding photos, i.e., traditional, artsy, casual, funky, sexy, etc. What do you say?

❧

What are the best and worst wedding trends out there right now?

❧

Together you have agreed to give up one thing for marriage. What will it be for each of you?

What is the biggest outstanding issue to solve
before the wedding day?

You need your groom to be more enthusiastic about one thing regarding the planning of the wedding. What?

~

You need your bride to be less enthusiastic about what?

~

Your fiancé tells you, "The pet goes or I do." What's your decision?

~

What for you are the pros and cons of a joint wedding shower with both the bride and groom?

~

Who will the flower girls be and what do you have in mind for the dresses?

If you could have your fiancé say any one thing to your parents the morning of the wedding, what would you like it to be?

If you could play matchmaker with your wedding guests, who would you hook up?

❧

Your best man, or maid of honor, tells you they have a crush on your fiancé. What now?

❧

If someone started to dish the dirt on your fiancé's previous romantic history at the reception, what would you say to them?

❧

Pimp My Wheels is going to customize a wedding mobile just for you. What do you want it to feature?

❧

What one thing do you want to continue to do only by yourself even after marriage?

You want a perfect and relaxing evening the
night before the wedding to help you sleep
well. What does it entail?

The best advice you have been given so far regarding planning a wedding has been . . . ?

∼

You are praying that on your wedding day your fiancé does *not* do one thing he/she always does. And that is?

∼

If your engagement period could be as romantic as any film, which film would it be?

∼

If you could drive off into the sunset after your wedding party in any kind of vehicle, what kind would it be, and who would drive?

The thing you love about your fiancé and want

everyone to know is . . . ?

Finances aside, if you could decorate with any flowers, in any color, that somehow reflect perfectly the two of you, which would they be?

❧

You discover your beautiful engagement ring is a conflict diamond. What do you do?

❧

If you were to plan your own perfect bachelorette party, where would you go, and what would you do?

❧

You dream of a romantic, tranquil place for your honeymoon, but your groom really wants to go to Disney World. How do you come to an agreement?

You discover that your fiancé has a huge debt load you never knew about. What now? You discover that your fiancé has a huge amount of money saved in a Swiss bank and has not mentioned it. Do you say anything?

If you could release anything into the sky right after the ceremony, what would it be?

❧

For you, the best thing and the worst thing about being single is . . . ?

❧

If you could select and coordinate all the jewelry of those participating in the wedding, what would it look like?

❧

If a wedding is really all about two people in love, does it matter what they wear?

❧

How will this wedding change your career?

If you were to choose the accessories that are a "must" at your wedding party, and those which are banned, what would they be for each?

Will you be concerned that everyone's having a good time at your reception, or will you be totally focused on your new spouse?

❧

Your engagement is going to be filmed as a love story. What actors should play the parts of each of you?

❧

If you could have the stylist of any actress all to yourself to prepare you for the day, whose would you choose?

❧

If you were to name the three top songs in the running for the first dance, what would they be?

❧

If you left the choice of first-dance song to your fiancé, what would he/she pick?

If your groom told you he wanted to
completely change his look for the wedding,
what would you suggest he do?

Your future spouse just told you his/her parents won't pay
for any part of the wedding. How do you respond?

⌒

A study proves that couples that do premarital counseling
have a much better chance of making the marriage last,
and your fiancé wants to do it. What is your reaction?

⌒

You have someone in mind to catch the bouquet and
the garter. Who?

⌒

What has been the nastiest pre-wedding fight thus far?

⌒

Your fiancé has told you that he/she wants to forget the
whole wedding affair and elope. How do you react?

If you were to name the wedding tradition you
most love, and the one you most hate, what
would it be for each?

For the *continuity of life,* what "something old"
will you choose?

❧

For your *promise of a new life,* what "something new"
will you pick?

❧

For "something borrowed," you want to ask *who,*
for *what*?

To symbolize your <u>purity of heart</u>, your
"something blue" will be . . . ?

Your best friend gives you an offensively cheap gift. Do you say anything?

❧

If you could have any gift from the mother of the bride, what would you want?

❧

What is the ideal length of a toast, and what topic should always be avoided?

❧

Some of the guests decide not to sit at their assigned seats. How do you deal with it?

❧

You find out that some not-so-close friends are offended they haven't been asked as bridesmaids or groomsmen. Should you worry about it?

An expensive wedding gift arrives from an "ex" who is decidedly not invited to the wedding. Now what?

If you could give your mother any advice regarding her wedding day attire, and have her follow it, what would you say?

❧

On a scale of 1 to 100 percent, how sure are you that you are marrying the right person?

❧

Who do you predict will do the most embarrassing thing at the wedding?

❧

While powdering your nose you overhear a catty conversation about your wedding dress. What's the worst thing they could say?

❧

All of your married friends say sexual passion doesn't survive marriage. Do you believe them?

If you were to draw the line between flirting and cheating, now that you are engaged, what would it be for each of you?

If you were to predict how your life will change most
after the wedding, what would you say?

❦

What is the destination wedding of your dreams?

❦

You are offered the chance to get married in any sports
stadium, wearing any team uniform. Where would
you do it?

❦

Do you think siblings should have automatic rank over
friends in the wedding party?

❦

If one future in-law had to be the one to compose your
vows, who would you choose?

If you could avoid a specific "bridezilla" characteristic, which would it be and how would you avoid it?

You are determined not to fall into the classic role of "detached groom," so you will avoid it by doing what?

Your mother-in-law-to-be constantly talks
about the "ex" and you are afraid she will
"blab on" at the wedding. Do you say something?

❦

You want every out-of-town guest to have a welcome gift
basket waiting for them at their accommodations.
What things will you put in it?

❦

If you could have anything hidden in the wedding cake,
what would you put in there?

❦

If you wanted to surprise your groom with a special
food treat at the reception, what would it be?

If you could make sure that your fiancé does one thing for sure at the stag or bachelorette party, and does <u>not</u> do one thing normally done, what would they be?

In what way has your relationship with your parents changed since you became engaged?

❧

You have one idea for the style of the wedding; your fiancé has another. How do they compare and contrast?

❧

You would like to put one thing on every guest's table to help get the conversation going during the wedding. What could it be?

❧

After the ceremony you change into the dress for the reception, only to find your new sister-in-law wearing the identical dress. Now what?

There is one thing that you hope people will say
about your wedding the day after,
and it is . . . ?
If there is one thing you do not want people
to say about your wedding afterward,
what would it be?

What does a "glowing bride" mean to you?

❧

You have decided it would be romantic to abstain from
physical relations for a period leading up to the
big day, to make the wedding night extra special.
How long do you remain celibate?

❧

If one routine thing you do now as boyfriend and
girlfriend could always be part of your life,
what would you like it to be?

❧

You have had to compromise on some things regarding
the wedding, and the one compromise you are not
happy with is what?

A network wants to make a reality TV show about your engagement. What title would best describe the show?

You get to pick out any kind of lingerie for your bride to wear under her wedding dress. What do you want it to look like?

❧

If you were to name your best online source so far, which would it be?

❧

For you, what will make being a "newlywed" better than being a seasoned married couple?

❧

If there's one thing you've learned so far about planning a wedding, by way of giving advice, what would you say it is?

What one thing will make your wedding
different from all others?

Your fiancé declares that his/her mother has final say over the guest list and that is that. What do you have to say about it?

❧

If you could have any author/writer compose your wedding vows, who would you pick?

❧

What one material object best expresses love to you?

❧

If you could have anything or everything monogrammed for the wedding, what items would you have done and how would it be designed?

When will the moment of wedding bliss
fall upon you?

The wedding theme just right for you is . . . ?
The theme for your fiancé?

❧

What will the dog wear?

❧

Looming out there is one unspoken issue regarding
the wedding that you are both avoiding.
What is it?

❧

If there's one thing about marrying that people should be
better at the second time around, what would it be?

You find out that your fiancé has included an old flame on the invitation list. What do you do?

You rewrite "until death do us part," replacing it with . . .

❧

If you were to state the terms of the perfect prenuptial, what would they be?

❧

In your words, what are the duties of the best man and bridesmaid, and what in particular would you like them to do for you?

❧

You want to agree now about how, where, and with whom you will spend the holidays between the two families. What do you propose?

What aspect of this commitment will change your life the most?

If your betrothed insisted that you raise your children in a faith other than yours, what would you do?

❧

Your boss hints that he/she expects to be invited to the wedding, but you weren't planning to. Now what?

❧

Your fiancé really wants a cheap, at-home ceremony. What do you do?

❧

Some of your friends tell you to keep your own last name after marriage, and others advise you to take your husband's. What are your thoughts?

You get to choose a wedding gift that cannot be bought with money. What do you ask for?

For someone waiting for this day their whole life, is there such a thing as a wedding that's too expensive?

❧

If you could be bolder in one area regarding the whole engagement process and wedding planning, in what area would it be?

❧

You get to dedicate your wedding to someone other than yourselves. Who do you choose?

❧

Your in-laws have proposed that they will pay for your honeymoon and that you can go anywhere you like, do anything you like, and stay as long as you like, but they get to come along. What is your answer?

You decide to spend a splurge weekend away with your best friends before the wedding. Where would you go and what would you do?

If you could send a big glossy photo from your wedding to someone from your past, just to spite them, who would you mail it to?

❧

You would like your in-laws and parents to coordinate one thing beautifully. What do you hope it to be?

❧

Your friends want to know your secret to success for "popping the question." What do you tell them?

❧

A number of trusted friends kindly warn you not to go through with this marriage and want to stop it. What do you do?

How would you finish the phrase
"Just for that day, I wish . . ."?

If you could secretly carry one small thing during your wedding ceremony, what would it be?

❧

You would love to modify one thing about the place you have chosen for the wedding reception. What do you change?

❧

If you could have any star's plastic surgeon do a little alteration before the big day, whose doctor would you pick and what would you have done?

❧

Your fiancé starts packing on the pounds a couple of months before the wedding. What do you say to him/her?

Your maid of honor has dropped the ball on you and is not getting anything planned or done. How do you handle it?

$\mathcal{W}hat$ is the next big event that you hope will happen after the wedding?

∽

$\mathcal{A}$ psychic strongly recommends changing the date of the wedding, but the invitations have already been printed. What now?

∽

$\mathcal{Y}our$ fiancé tells you to have a fling before the wedding night, as long as he/she can too. How do you react?

How do you foresee coordinating your respective religious traditions into the ceremony?

You have the chance to bring back one deceased relative or friend just for your wedding day. Who do you pick?

❧

The kinkiest thing you would do on your honeymoon is . . .

❧

What are the three most important things that you as a couple have agreed to spend your money on?

❧

It comes to light that one of you would be willing to adopt kids, and that one of you would not. How does this affect the engagement?

The person who is making the wedding planning
most difficult is . . . And the most helpful?

If you could pay money to restore your virginity before your wedding day, how much would you be willing to cough up? How much would your fiancé kick in?

❧

How would you finish the phrase, "I was a great catch because . . ."?

❧

If you were to name one way in which your fiancé is least like others of his/her gender, what would you say?

❧

If you could have proposed to your fiancé in any way, meaning the sky is the limit, how would you have done it?

Has being engaged made you nostalgic
for anything?

You want to switch one thing from your wedding "to do" list with something from your fiancé's. What would you trade?

❧

If creating the wedding of your dreams meant delaying a house purchase for a few years, what would you do?

❧

What would you do differently if you had twice as much time to plan your wedding?

❧

If you could cast off, for good, any one fear you have before tying the knot, what would it be?

What has been your most romantic time
together thus far?

If you could exchange tattoos instead of rings, what design would you pick for each other and where would you put them?

❧

What is the funniest wedding blooper you have ever seen?

❧

If you could treat yourself to a whole day at a relaxing spa before the wedding, what treatments would you ask for?

❧

The marital trap you want to avoid most is . . . ?

What is the one "deal breaker" regarding this engagement?

How will you know when the dress you find is right
for you?

∾

You will need someone to turn and talk to during this
pre-wedding buildup. Who will you trust most to
listen and to give you good advice?

∾

People say that too much routine kills the romance
in a relationship after you are married. How will
you deal with this?

What wedding expense would get cut first if
you were over budget? Which is untouchable?

You want the color scheme for the reception to best
reflect the both of you. What colors would
be accurate?

❧

If your groom could be as attractive as any famous person
just for the big day, who would it be?

❧

If your bride could be as elegant as any famous woman
for the wedding, who would she be like?

❧

If you were to name a point in the relationship when
you thought it just might not work, when would
it have been?

How would you complete the phrase
"A life without love..."

You learn that one set of parents is planning to give an overly generous gift that you fear will upset the other set of parents. How do you handle it?

❧

What one thing are you ready to compromise, and what one thing will you never compromise, once you are married?

❧

Your groom wants to show you the videotapes of his decadent bachelor party before the wedding day. Will you watch?

❧

You have noticed a whole lot of text messages from the former lover on your fiancée's phone since you got engaged. What do you do?

You get to do one last thing before your
wedding day without your fiancé ever knowing.
What should it be?

What things must match with regard to attire and decor?

❧

If you had a wedding planner, in what areas would you give them total control, and which part would you keep control of yourself?

❧

How long do you predict you will go before your first post-wedding fight?

❧

What would you never say to your fiancé about his/her parents?

What one thing gets you worked up most
quickly regarding planning the wedding?

What would you do if, about a month before the wedding, your fiancé vanished for two days without an explanation, refusing to discuss it?

❧

You have found out that someone not invited to the wedding was invited to the bridal shower, or vice versa. How do you solve it?

❧

If you were to put a monetary limit on what the bridesmaids should spend overall, what would it be?

For you, the perfect division of costs for the
whole affair should be . . . ?

What shoes do you just have to have going down the aisle?

❧

The one value you know that you both must have in common before you would even consider getting married is . . .

❧

If there was one thing you wish you didn't know about your betrothed before marrying, what would it be?

❧

Your spouse-to-be has asked you the question you never wanted to answer. What was the question?

What one superstition do you have about the
wedding day?

How should a second marriage and ceremony differ
from a first marriage?

∽

If you discovered by chance that your fiancé had been
married before but didn't tell you, how would
you react?

∽

Your fiancé gets cold feet: what do you do about it?

∽

You and your fiancé agree to disagree about one topic,
even after you are married. What is it?

What will be your mantra for getting through
the planning of the big day?

You've lost your engagement ring. What do you tell your fiancé?

❧

If you were to quantify how much time you will spend organizing the wedding versus your fiancé, what would it be for each?

❧

What part of the limelight will you revel in during the months you are a bride-to-be?

❧

At the moment you say "I do," what will be your dominant emotion?

They say there is no such thing as a perfect spouse, just the perfect spouse <u>for you</u>. How is this true in your case?

About the Authors

Evelyn McFarlane was born in New York. She studied architecture in New York and painting in Italy. She currently lives in Florence, Italy, where she writes and paints, and she is the mother of a seven-year-old child.

James Saywell is an architect and writer living in Hong Kong and Tuscany.